A PUFF OF SMOKE

Also by Sarah Lippett:

Stan and Nan

A PUFF OF SMOKE

Sarah Lippett

Jonathan Cape
LONDON

For Mum and Dad

A PUFF OF SMOKE

I.

my little sisters

I don't remember much before it happened.

I have a few vague memories, but I'm not sure anymore if I made them up.

I do remember my little sister.

She was the smallest purple person I have ever seen.

I kept thinking — how could a little purple person resemble me?

It seemed like Mum cried every day for that year.

Everyone said that if she'd lived,
she would of looked like me.

She tried to find comfort
at church but they
couldn't provide
any answers.

God gives
and God
takes.

At home things weren't quite the same.

Dad was usually the one with the short temper. If he told us to go to bed, we'd go to bed...

...no questions asked.

ALL BALL GAMES ARE PROHIBITED

Town Clerk

But that year, the year of Mum's deep sadness...

...she was the one who seemed to snap at us for no reason.

We were kids. We didn't understand death.

We were kids. We didn't understand death.

We didn't understand how you could cry for someone who had never 'lived'.

Months passed and not much changed...

CHEPSTOW DRIVE

...until the Autumn.

october

Mum was back to her old self again.

November

It's not fair.

December

Julie! Let Zoe help.

We waited patiently for a new sibling.

January

February

MICK!

March

I'll call when we have news.

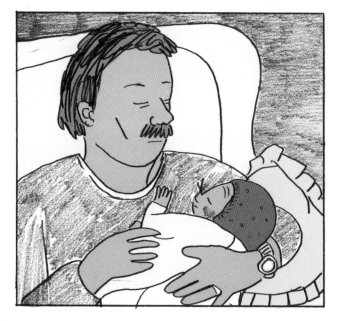
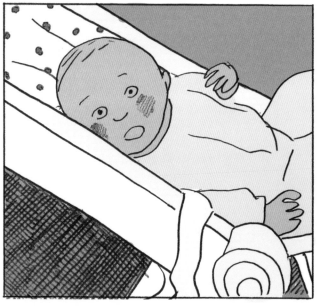

We only have one video of us as a family. It was made in 1992 at my dad's birthday party.

My uncle brought round a video camera...

5:28 PM
APR 25 1992

Everyone was begging for the attention of the cameraman...

oh! Don't film me!

THE CURE · DISINTEGRATION

WAHOO!

SteelyDan

'REELING IN THE YEARS'

Whoosh!

JULIE! IF THAT'S SCRATCHED...

Haha!... Er...only joking!

There are times when the camera pans on me...

...where perhaps you could tell something was wrong.

All I really remember is that I adored being a big sister...

...I loved Samantha.

But that I didn't feel quite the same as I used to.

I lived in Stafford, in the midlands.
Our house was in a quiet part of the town
called Wildwood.

WAIL!

Shhh now, Sammy...

The house was always noisy and trying to get a word in at any time was difficult, but I loved it.

Stop it!

I said... STOP IT!

THAT'S ENOUGH!

JULIE. GO AND EAT IN THE KITCHEN. ZOE... I DON'T WANT TO HEAR A WORD.

IT'S NOT FAIR!

SMASH!!

Sarah!

You don't need to break things for attention, Sarah. I love you all the same.

I'm sorry.

I was a popular kid at school.

SARAH!

And although I was quiet, the other kids didn't seem to mind.

Don't talk to her.

She doesn't like you.

GO AWAY!

Did you know that if you kiss a boy, you'll have a baby?

EW!

The buildings at school were made of this strange bobble-like concrete.

My friends and I would imagine it was once an alien's fortress until some teachers tranformed it into a school.

When the headaches started I would stand alone along a different side of the building.

I would place my forehead against the wall, pressing the cold sharp bobbles into my skin...

...believing that the aliens who had built the school would make the pain go away.

I continued trying to be me. I went to my dancing classes...

...brownies...

...and school.

I thought about telling mum and dad about the pain in my head...

...but I didn't think they'd believe me.

I kept thinking...

I must be making this up...

Maybe it's all in my mind.

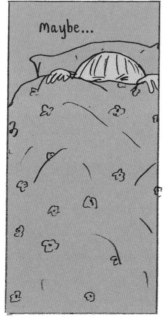

Maybe...

...maybe everyone feels like this...

2.

Losing Control

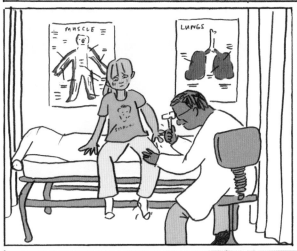
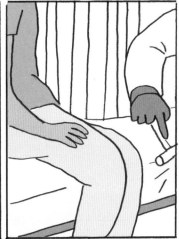

You need to take Sarah to the hospital straight away...

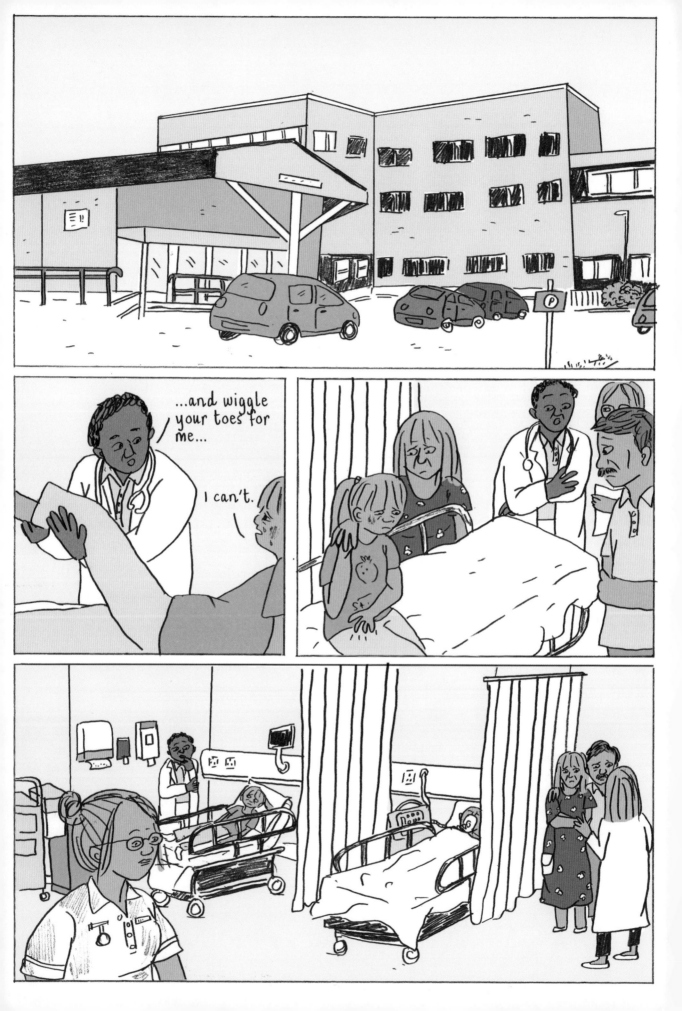

Look at the animals, Sarah!

SWISH SWISH

SWISH SWISH

SLOSH! SLOSH!

What's wrong, sweetie?

My Mum said she'd be back to see me but she's not here.

She'll be here soon, my dear. It's still very early.

Morning, Sarah!

Oh! Look! Here comes your breakfast

Yum! That toast looks tasty!

The toast didn't taste like my toast at home.

...and it smelt the same as my bear did.

Try and eat a little bit more.

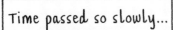
Time passed so slowly...

It was the first time in my life I'd been left alone.

I was positive mum and dad would never return.

The hospital blankets are too rough on Sarah's skin. She's getting sores.

It might be an idea to bring in her duvet or a soft blanket.

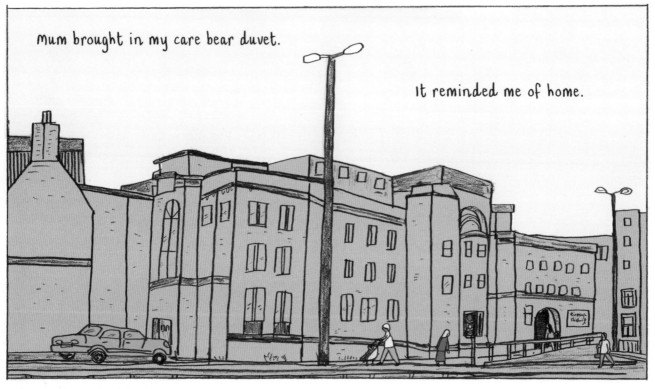

Mum brought in my care bear duvet.

It reminded me of home.

I could almost pretend...

...that I was back in my own bed...

...back where I belonged.

Hey, how's my Ses?*

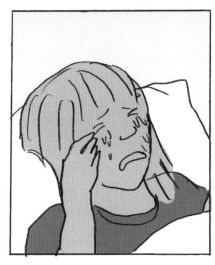

You'll be home soon.

The doctors just need to find out what's wrong and get you on the mend.

Every day Mum brought me a can of Fanta from the machine downstairs.

It was so cold on my throat, so sweet... I imagined how jealous Zoe would be.

IT'S NOT FAIR!

* Ses is my dad's nickname for me. Neither of us can remember its' origins.

I wasn't fond of the hospital food.

Oooh! That looks nice... Scrambled eggs?

It's mac 'n' cheese, mum...

I only had an appetite for their puddings

There's arctic roll or jelly and ice cream.

Mum and dad brought in dinner from home for me.

You'll enjoy this!

The plate and its contents took me back...

...back to the noisy dinners, squabbles... my family.

JULIE!

I REFUSE TO EAT COW!

Good to see you eating, Sarah!

When you're done we'll need to take some blood.

...And now for a little test...

Your mum will be with you the whole time.

Hello, Sarah, my name's Prof.G.

Say hello, Ses.

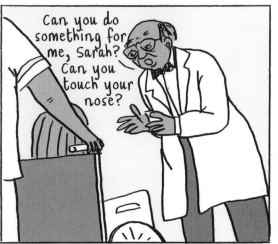

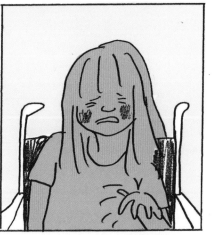

I missed my sisters.

And I missed my brother.

Do you think she'll be okay?

I don't know.

So what's the diagnosis?!

We think that Sarah may have a brain tumour.

Don't worry, don't worry...

...It's going to be okay.

3.

Some kind of diagnosis

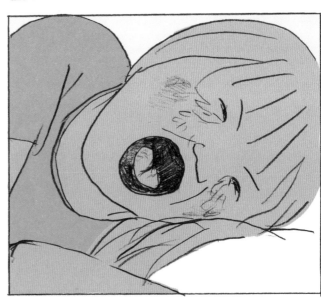

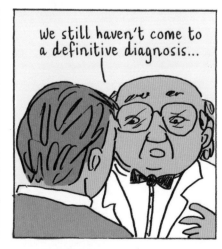

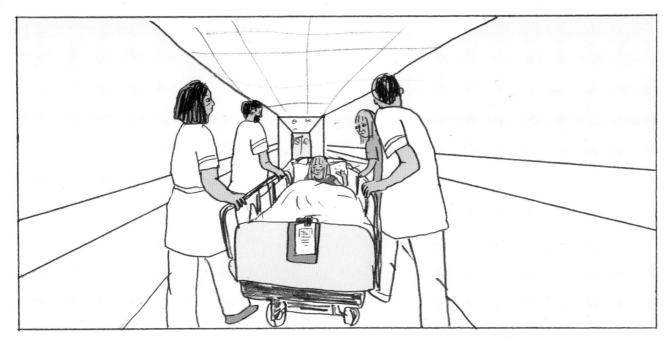

It was better on the ward.

I had two neighbours. A boy around my age...

GET WELL

...and a little girl about three years old.

This is Natasha. The hospital are letting her come home for the weekend...it's her first time at home. She's spent her whole life in hospital.

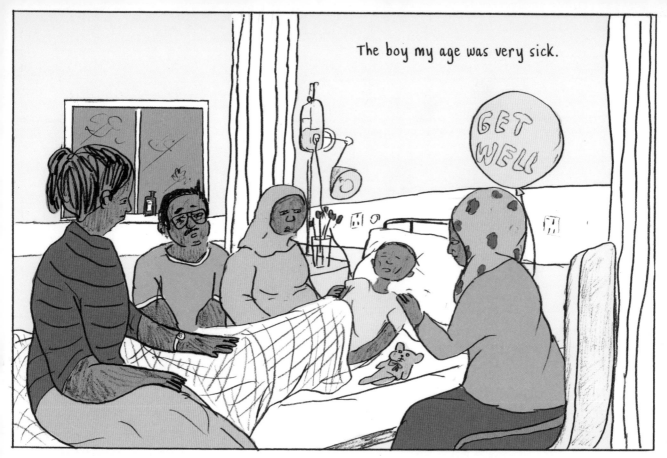

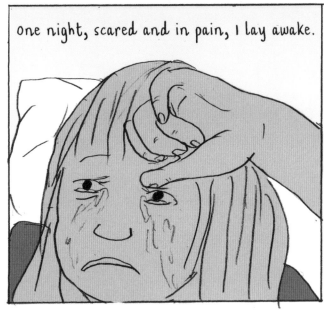

one night, scared and in pain, I lay awake.

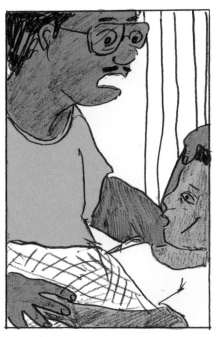

Morning Sarah!

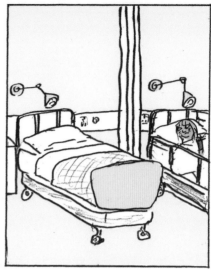

A day or so later, I had a new neighbour...

...and a diagnosis.

The good news is we know what's wrong.

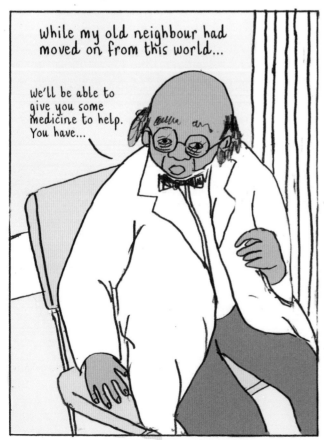

While my old neighbour had moved on from this world...

We'll be able to give you some medicine to help. You have...

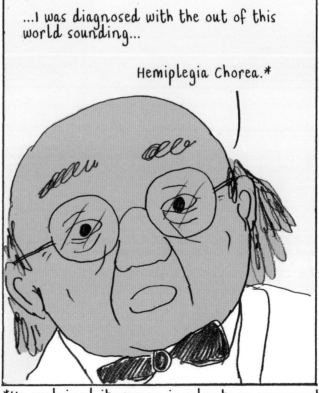

...I was diagnosed with the out of this world sounding...

Hemiplegia Chorea.*

*He explained it was an involuntary movement disorder that could be controlled with medicine

4.

Home

I came home to piles of get well cards from strangers and a basket of fruit from the local grocers.

oh, look, Ses!

The fruit made me angry.

Why would someone give fruit to a kid as a gift!?

I couldn't walk.

Up we go!

Everyone enjoyed pushing me in my chair.

Careful, Zoe!

The 'Fellowship', a local Christian group, made several apperances in an attempt to 'save' me.

oh...hello Jill, Cathy...

How's Sarah?

Getting there...

We'd like to help...

...to help Sarah.

She has plenty of help.

We believe the devil is inside Sarah... that's why she's so ill.

There's a great priest coming to town. He'll place his hands on her to drive the devil OUT!

No thank you...

Mum and I would go for walks down the local fields, and along the canal.

We would make charts, counting the narrow boats, and marking them out of ten for their friendliness and the presentation of their boat.

She's just through here.

I had a home school teacher, Mrs Emms. She was a lot older than my teachers at school.

It was hard to concentrate, to add and multiply.

But Mrs Emms was kind and patient.

...Plus she showed an interest in my troll collection.

This one has funky hair... ...doesn't he?

He's called Buster.

Dinner time was a challenge. My left arm lay weak and motionless.

I couldn't cut up my food, but it didn't bother anyone at the table.

After some medication changes and physio...

...I could walk again and what remained of my illness I found ways to hide.

I saw Dr. W in Birmingham.

Let's increase the dosage...

And Dr. C in Stafford.

When I go to the toilet... it..erm...

MUMMY!!! IT HURTS!!!

I think Sarah might have another infection.

Yes. It looks like you do. Let's take some bloods.

And I think Sarah, you should see a renal specialist.

Are you okay with needles, Sarah?

Yes.

Wow. A few of my adult patients should see how brave you are!

They'd be running out the door by now.

I returned to school just under a year later, but things were different.

I still wasn't well.

Sarah?

Often still too sick to go to school. I was a ghost of my former self.

Most people had forgotten me.

It's on Saturday.

But Kathryn hadn't.

Kathryn's invited me to her party!

How exciting!

Thanks for inviting Sarah.

It's been such a difficult year for her.

oh...well...there must have been a mistake.

Ah, well, we can't have Sarah at the party...

Kathryn wrote the invites but erm... I don't want illness in my house...

We just can't be doing with illness in my house

Luckily, being one of five...

...there was always someone to spend time with...

...no matter how many friends I didn't have at school.

And more changes came along. I was now a glasses wearer.

Okay, Sarah. Read as many lines as you can for me.

Zoë gave me a new nickname.

Hi, glasses woman.

I regularly had EEGs' or Electroencephalography to be precise.

It was a test that recorded my brain activity. The technician placed small sensors on my scalp with sticky glue.

Sarah Lippett?

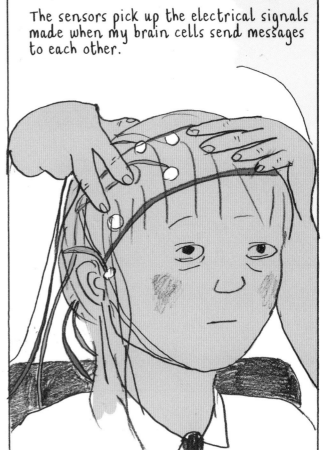

The sensors pick up the electrical signals made when my brain cells send messages to each other.

They were looking for unusual activity that would explain my symptoms.

Ses, you look like Davros from Dr Who!

I had this test many times.

Hmm. I think we should do a sleep deprived EEG.

There may be more chance of us finding abnormal activity linked to Sarah's symptoms.

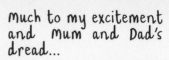

Much to my excitement and Mum and Dad's dread...

...I was to stay awake all night.

Mum and Dad took it in turns to keep me awake.

Everything seemed different, exciting.

MUM! THE MILK MAN'S HERE!

That's great, Sarah.

mum! mum! LOOK!

It was the first time I'd ever seen a sunrise and it was beautiful!

Sarah! Wake up!

Come on! We've got to go...

I also had 48 hour EEGs'.

My Secretary will send that over to you...

They gave me a walkman style recorder...

Now, where did we park?

...in an ancient leather bag that all the electrodes were attached to.

Mum said I was allowed to stay off school.

Bye Dad!

Just in case one of the kids knocked my head gear...

Sam, don't eat the crayons.

...plus I don't think she wanted anyone to see me!

Mum?

Yes dear? WAAA!

Can I post my letter to Nan?

Of course. Pop a stamp on it.

I was desperate to walk outside of the house, for someone from school, anyone, to see me. I wanted the attention.

For the kids at school to notice me, for them to have a reason to speak to me.

5.

Rumpelstiltskin

YOU'D CALL CHILDLINE! WOULDN'T YOU?

SOB SOB SOB

Have you heard of Childline, Sarah?...

WHAT THE HELL IS GOING ON?!

I'm sorry, Sarah. I'm sorry...

The doctors had jumped to conclusions.

The usual conclusions you'd come to...

...if presented with a depressed child with urine infections.

I can't believe what they tried to insinuate.

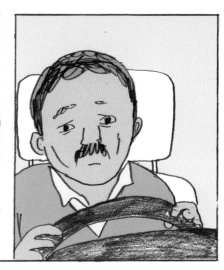

The experience was a lasting one that left me with a chronic fear of psychologists.

...complete waste of time...

We don't need their help.

At school I was behind. Separated from my old friends, I was moved to the table with the other struggling kids.

I had to sit next to Richard A and Vicky B.

I longed to be back at my old table.

I didn't want to be one of <u>those</u> kids.

Mrs J, our teacher, was pretty and kind.

She had long dainty fingers which she used to explain or tell us stories which required emphasis.

I like Mrs J.

Me too.

Sarah!

DUMBO

During the holidays Mrs J gave me extra homework...

In a minute, mum!

...so I could catch up.

It's time to do your homework!

I KNOW! I'M COMING!

MUM! I can't do it...

During the last term of my first year back at school, auditions were held as usual for the parts in the summer play. That year it was Rumpelstiltskin.

The King says I... must...spin...straw into gold or erm...

...I must die.

Very good, Rebecca. Next, Sarah Lippett.

I saw the audition as a chance for me to be good at something, a chance for me to be noticed.

What's next?

Rehearsals were every afternoon during the run-up to the play. I practised my lines regularly.

I was enjoying myself so much.

And then I say...

I almost forgot I was sick.

...but I have nothing left to give!

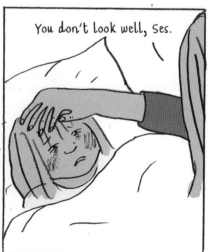

You don't look well, Ses.

I can't miss rehearsal.

You can't go to school like this. Sorry, Ses.

When is Sarah going to play?

Mum! I can still remember my lines!

Hi Holly!

oh.. hi... You're back.

It's nice to see you back, Sarah. How're you feeling?

Better.

You still have your part in the play if you want it... But while you were away...

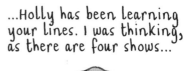

...Holly has been learning your lines. I was thinking, as there are four shows...

...perhaps you and Holly could share the part?

You can play the part for for two shows... and... Holly can play the part for two...

How do you feel about that? Is that okay?

NOOOOO!

Yes. okay.

Show time came around quickly and I was determined to play my part...

Once upon a time there was a miller who boasted that his daughter could spin straw into gold...

Now get to work. Spin this straw into gold.

Oh no!

The King says I must turn straw into gold or I must die...

I CAN HELP YOU!

...But only if you give me something in return...

Here, take my necklace.

6.

The Accident

I had a new doctor. Dr.H. She was South African and she put me on a regular antibiotic called Cefalexin.

Dad liked it when she said Cefalexin in her accent.

I didn't like that Dad liked the way Dr.H said Cefalexin in her accent.

For seven days, before breakfast, I had to do a urine sample.

Another one done!

Mum stored them in the fridge.

Ew! What's that Mum?!

oh, it's just Sarah's urine samples. We have to store them there until your dad can take them to the hospital lab.

Haha!

You're so gross!

Summer 1995

Mick. We need to food shop tonight, and pick up Zoe from her piano lesson...

...oh and you need to drop Julie at her party at 8...

Hi, daddy!

Okay, Lesley...

Hello, Sammy!

Hello, daddy!

What ya drawin', Sawah?

Dad's feet! Haha!

I'm too hot!

me too.

My health was now relatively stable and life seemed to be getting better, more routine.

But as it turned out...

...the peace doesn't last long in our family.

Sammy! Get that shoe off!

It was June, the start of Summer and it was a hot one.

So what's going on?

We only knew what mum and dad told us.

She's in a coma.

The doctors don't know right now whether she'll come round...

..and if she does, whether she'll still be Julie...

I'm sorry.

She'll be okay, dad.

...because she's Julie...

Teachers and parents at school kept asking how Julie was doing. It was a big story in the local news.

That's Julie's sister.

Mum said that when she was with Julie, surrounded by paramedics and locals, Mrs D, a teacher at school whom we all knew, kept saying sorry. Mum didn't understand why at the time.

Julie had got off the bus, and run across the road at the end of our street. She had crossed without looking, just as our teacher drove around the corner.

The whole bus had been witnesses...

...including the driver...who having had a front row seat for the spectacle...

...had taken a month's leave from work with stress and anxiety.

Every day when I walked to school I saw Julie's dry blood in the road. It was a constant reminder.

CHEPSTOW DRIVE

I couldn't cross that road for years after it happened.

I used the scary-looking underpass... ...Anything to avoid that road.

Weeks went by, and card after card was posted through our door by strangers. Mum hung them up on string like she did at Christmas.

Everyone wanted to know how she was doing...

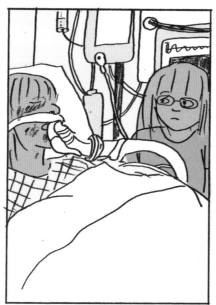

And then one day, some time later...

...she woke up. And she was still Julie.

Julie!

Haha!

What's happening in Neighbours?

Haha!

Julie quickly recovered. Our family holiday had been cancelled during her unstable period and it made me angry.

Hi Ju.

Hey Sarah!

IT'S NOT FAIR, MUM!

Why can't we re-book the holiday?!

It's too late now Ses.

But mainly I was grateful that Julie was okay and that the accident hadn't happened to me.

What's that?

It's Turps. I use it to clean my brushes.

It stinks!

The summer ended. Mark went back to University, Julie started College and I started High School It was a new chapter.

7.

A New Start

I was feeling more optimistic.

High School was a fresh start.

Look out for Sarah, Zoe!

I saw it as a chance for me to make new friends.

I WILL, mum!

And to be cool.

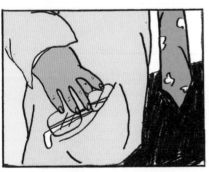

Hey, Sarah!

Oh, hi Hayley!

Where are your glasses?

Oh, I don't need to wear them all the time.

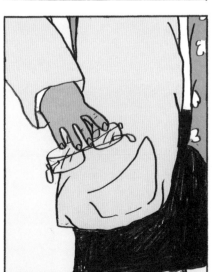

Hey, Sarah! It's Sarah, isn't it?

oh hi, Katie!

Are you walking this way? Where do you live?

Yeah. I live in Wildwood.

Cool. I'm not far... on Knowle Road.

So.. what erm do you think of Walton so far?

It's okay.

Hayley's pretty annoying right? She's obsessed with NSYNC. I don't even like them.

Me neither!

YOU HAVE TEN NEW MESSAGES...

...AND TWENTY SAVED MESSAGES.

I made a new friend at school yesterday...

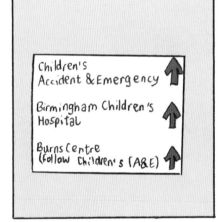

Fatty tissue again.

We're going in one more time.

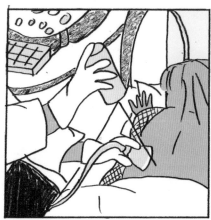

Fatty tissue.

This should be it, Sarah.

We've got it!

You did so well, Sarah.

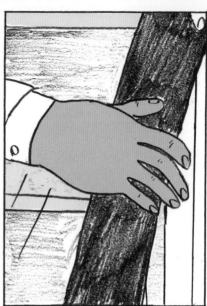

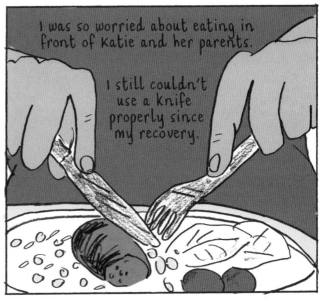

8.

Side Effects

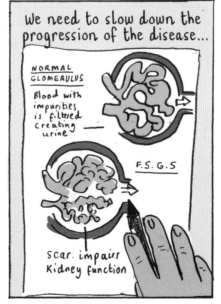

There were a few options of medications
Dr H wanted to try.

Each of them had side effects.

They included growing facial hair..

...growing thick gums...

... infertility...

There was one medication that would make me
gain a lot of weight...

And one that would make my hair fall out.

I went into hospital every six weeks for three sessions of intraveneous treatment of cyclophosphamide.

My name's Alison. I'll be taking care of you today

Which hand would you like your canular in?

Left please, so I can draw.

I feel terrible..

Oh, Ses...

The day was always a long one...

And I'd feel sicker and sicker until it was time to leave.

Whatever you do, don't let them give you steroids or you could end up as fat as me...

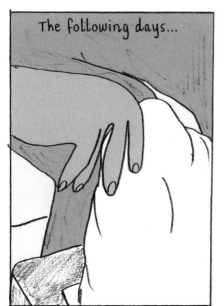

The following days...

...were mainly spent beside a bucket or a toilet.

Once I'd recovered, I'd have an amazing lease of life until the next instalment.

OI LIPPETT!

Is your hair naturally blonde or do you dye it?

WHAT?! It's natural!

LET ME SEE!

YANK!

ARGGHH

Whaaa!? How come yer hair just comes out like that?

When I was in the hospital, it was easier to have perspective. There was always someone sat next to you that at least looked worse off than you...

...but when I was back at School, among the healthy, it felt harder to feel like I wasn't somehow being cheated.

9.

one step forward, two steps back

1998

My kidneys were stable.
My medicine was working.
But neurologically things had taken a turn for the worse.

It's not the Chorea. I know I don't have that anymore.

It's different.

I have pains down the left side of my body.

And headaches on the right side... here.

And she's tired all the time.

Yes. Extreme lethargy.

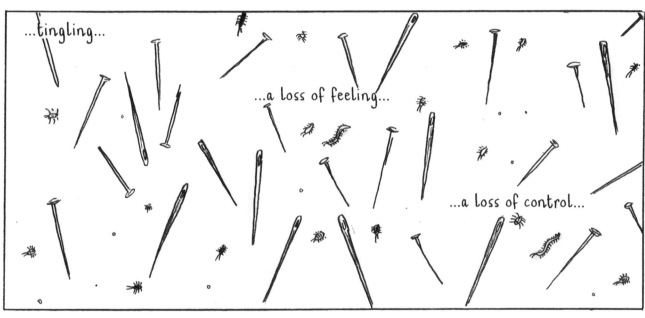

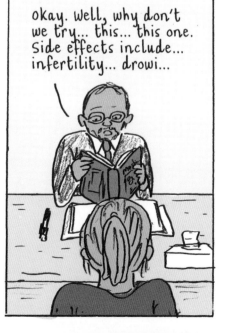

We were thinking that perhaps Sarah's and Heather's conditions...

...may have been caused by the chemicals that were used on the land...

...our houses were built on. It used to be farmland.

It's definitely something we should look into.

But again, there was nothing conclusive.

Well, there's no easy way to say this...

But...

...the results of your most recent MRI indicated...

...that you had a Stroke when you were seven...

...when you were first admitted.

It wasn't a surprise.

oh.

Mum and dad had always suspected that was what had happened years ago.

And so we laughed. There seemed nothing else to do but laugh.

So Dr C explained the results of the latest MRI?

So is Sarah at risk...?

Yeah. She did.

...of another Stroke? No, we don't think so...

The longer she doesn't have one, the less chance there is of her having another.

Shouldn't she be on blood thinners?!

Yes... that's a good idea.

With my symptoms worsening and the regularity of them increasing, my headaches became so severe I was spending days in bed, in the dark.

Mum described every symptom and how often they occured in a diary every day.

while they were living...

...I was merely existing.

This can't continue.
We need to call Dr W.

10.

Losing Faith

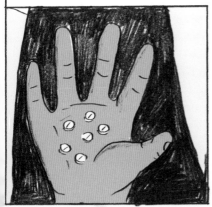

I can't get through to Dr. W. ...

I've left message after message with his secretary. ...Still nothing.

I was thinking, do you think maybe it's her medication?

Mick. Let's go.

Days turned into weeks. The ward was the most miserable place.

A few of us from the neurology ward went to the hospital school.

LIFT GOING DOWN.

This place is like a prison. I don't think they'll ever let us out.

That's Peter. He's on the psych ward.

My friend Katie would love him.

She loves Austin Powers!

I am a sexy beast!

Settle down, Peter. You're distracting everyone from their work.

oh! behave!

Dan and I would talk about what we would do once we were discharged and back in the outside world.

I'm going to eat a bean burger and chips!

We talked about the food we would eat...

I want pizza and cupcakes

...the friends we'd see...

My friend Jamie ate ten cupcakes in one go once!

...and the Nintendo games we'd play.

I'm going to play all my favourite Mario games and make my brother be Luigi!

...and my husband takes his medicine...

...at the same time every single day.

...he sets his watch to the right time...

Who's this?

...even when we're on holiday.

I don't know...

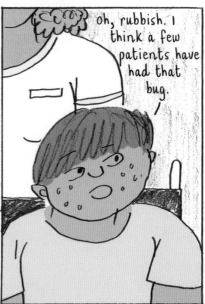

Haha! You've still got your hospital band on!

We stole you!

I'm stuffed. You better take me back to the prison.

Morning, Sarah!

It's just us today.

Where's Dan?

He's been moved to another ward.

Oh. Will he be at school?

I'm not sure.

A few days after my 'pizza break out', I was allowed to go home.

Dan's worst fears had been realised and he'd been moved down to the Psychiatric ward.

OI! LIPPETT!

YOU LOOK AS THIN AS A RAKE!

Thanks for your input, AARON.

I'm glad you're back.

I'm getting so stressed with all the coursework this term.

Me too. I'm so behind. I've been given some extensions but it's so hard to catch up..

Sat on the dining room carpet surrounded by Barbie, with pains in my arm and leg, something told me not to give up.

I don't know what it was, or why it should come to me in the middle of a game of Barbie with my little sister...

Perhaps it was some kind of higher power, but in that moment I knew I had to persevere, I couldn't give up.

I didn't know how I was going to get better...

...but I felt positive about my future for the first time in years.

Has anyone seen my dog?

II.

Boys and beer

I'd scraped together enough GCSE's to get into the Sixth Form at school. We celebrated our results at Ruth's — a girl in my year — house.

I don't think I'm gonna stay long.

How come? I don't really like these people.

They're alright. And the punch is good! Ha. I'm gonna go.

Still on for the Rose tonight?

Yeah! Bus there? Sure.

My dad will pick us up. Call ya! Cool!

The Red Rose was a run-down theatre where we went to watch out of town rock bands for a fiver on Friday nights.

They're really good.

I'M GONNA GET IN MY BIRTHDAY SUIT!

That's better. This last song is a Birthday Party cover... HIT IT!

I didn't expect that tonight.

Gross! Haha.

Hey...erm...Sarah?

"Still coming over tonight?"

The first year of Sixth Form was better because of Andy.

"Like, I was thinking what each of The Pixies' songs reminds me of..."

"What does 'Where Is My Mind' sound like?"

"Sounds like a factory where little men are making clogs."

"Haha!"

We went to gigs together in Birmingham.

You see that guy there? The one in the white tee drinking beer?

I think I know him.

I think I was in hospital with him, a year ago.

He couldn't walk then...but maybe he got better.

Shout his name.

DAN. DAN! DAN! DAN!

Hehe! He won't be able to hear you. Go over there!

Fine!

Excuse me. Sorry... Is your name Dan?

Nope.

Sorry. I thought you were someone I knew.

12.

The beginning of
the end

Listen, Ses. I don't want to talk about what happened.

Let's put it behind us.

...I am sorry. It won't happen again.

Last Friday

APOLLO CINEMAS

Thanks, Dad!

Final Fantasy was one of the most boring films I'd ever seen.

The party was amazing.

It was full of interesting University students
who were so much cooler than the people at school.

oh, erm... hey...

Hey.

Do you go to the Rose sometimes?

Yeah. I think I've seen you there occasionally ...with Katie?

Wanna get out of this chaos?

We can listen to some records.

Cool!

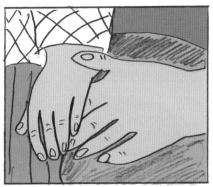

Here's your room. We'll do a 24 hour EEG first, and we'll be filming you too...so you'll be trapped in this room for a while...

Listen Ses, I'm going to head off. I've got a bit of business to do but I'll be back this afternoon.

She'll be fine with us.

Of course. Don't worry, dad.

There's a camp bed for your dad in the corner... and some blankets and pillows in the cupboard.

Thank you. He'll love that!

I listened to compilations Katie, Andy and my brother had made me.

I read the Electric Kool Aid Acid Test.

I imagined the freedom I'd feel
If I ever got better and went on a trip
with new and interesting friends...

Thats good thinking there, Cool Breeze
Cool Breeze is a Kid with three or four
beard sitting next to me on the stamped
metal bottom of the open back part of a
pickup truck. Bouncing along. Dipping
and rising and rolling on these ro ten s[?]
like a boat. Out the back of the truck th[?]
of San Francisco is bouncing down the
those endless staggers of bay windows
with a view bouncing and screaming d[?]
after another, electric signs with neon

...Blasting out the Grateful Dead and
singing at the top of our voices.

13.

Discovery

I started taking evening classes.

Mrs C gave me a reason to want to go to school.

She cared about what I was doing, and it made me care.

It's looking fantastic. So ambitious!

My old Maths teacher even came in to comment.

Anyone can do Maths. But not everyone can make Art. You have talent.

I don't know about that, Mr K, I feel the opposite. I'm useless at Maths.

I discovered new films, books, art and music.

He must be the only person in the world that hates The Beatles.

I spent hours copying CDs from the library on to cassette tapes.

I'd be too worried I'd get pregnant.

How did you get on at the hospital?

It was okay.

My new doctors thought they had a diagnosis. A diagnosis that would solve the mysteries of my medical past and present.

Way out

Feeling up to taking the stairs?

Ah, Sarah, you're awake. How are you feeling?

Erm... Where are my... pants?

The technician injected dye into your groin.....

...so you're going to feel a little tender and bruised down there.

We'll be monitoring you throughout the day and night.

You need to stay very flat. No walking around. Buzz me if you need the toilet.

The day I returned from London I was supposed to be resting.

SARAH! PHONE!

...but my brother called.

Oh hi, Mark.

They're showing 2001: A Space Odyssey tonight...

...at the cinema. It's worth seeing on the big screen. Wanna come?

I'm not supposed to be doing much, but the cinema can't hurt...

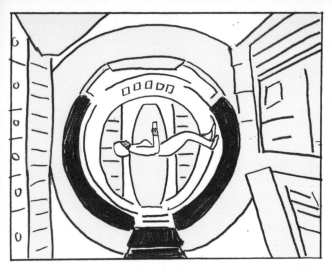

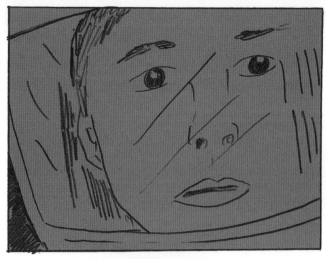

Bye, Dan!

I'm off into town.

Oh my God. That was possibly the best film I've ever seen.

Kubrick's good, isn't he?

Yeah. Thanks for inviting me.

It's cheered me up... James has...he's been acting strange lately.

And he's stopped calling me so much... He's probably busy with Uni work.

I guess I'm worried he's not cool about my health stuff.

He doesn't seem like that sort of person. Don't worry.

Yeah, I'm probably being paranoid.

Sarah! James is here!

Hey! Hello!

I bought you some camomile tea. It'll help with your mood.

WHAT?! You think I'm moody?!!!

Hey, I didn't mean it like that. I meant it was good for your stress...
How was the hospital?

The angiogram was weird...like...

...one minute I was wearing my gown... and my underwear.

Then after the procedure, I was naked apart from my gown.

Crazy.

So...I was thinking, we should go to Wolvey today. I want you to meet my mum.

Did you stay at James' last night then?

Yes, mum. And you let Zoe stay at her boyfriend's when she was my age...

I didn't say there was a problem.

..is it okay if I go to the festival for the whole weekend this year?

Do you think you'll manage?

I'll be fine. Plus Katie will be there.

I'll ask your dad. But it'll have to be your Birthday present.

Thank you mummy!

SUMMER 2002

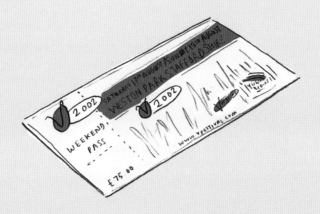

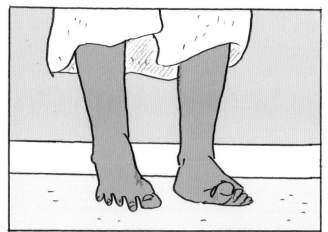

...James had broken up with me a couple of months before...

We need to talk.

I'm watching the film.

Come on, Sarah...

After we had broke up, James had quit University, met some girl and driven off into the abyss...

I was almost over it.

mum!

I got a place!

I'm so proud of you!

Well done, Sarah!

I can relax and enjoy the festival now!

Smiths okay?

Yeah. Definitely.

WHEN THE LEATHER RUNS SMOOTH ON THE PASSENGER SEAT!

I WOULD GO OUT TONIIIIGHT!

BUT I HAVEN'T GOT A STITCH TO WEAAAARRRRR!

SARAH!

14.

one in one million

So...

The hospital phoned— Great ormond Street...

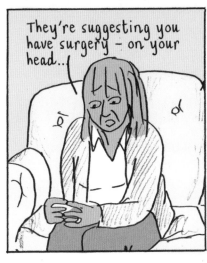

They're suggesting you have surgery - on your head...

W-What?!

They said that the angiogram, well, it showed abnormalities...

...in the tiny vessels...

...in your brain.

They believe the vessels..

...they're causing your symptoms.

Dr.G said...

...it's a very rare disease.

Effects one in one million.

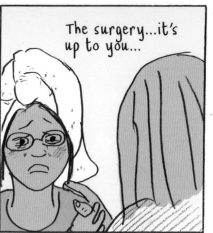

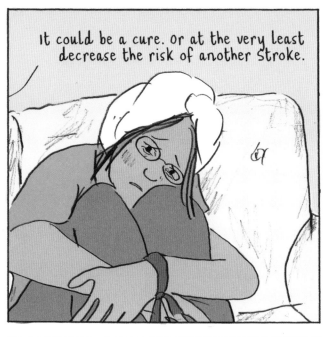

...It took a few days for the news to sink in. I didn't have the time to feel relief or validated by the news.

I talked to everyone in the family about their thoughts on the surgery.

The operation was booked for the end of October, during half term. I started college and I tried to forget about moyamoya and anything associated with it.

These drawings are wonderful... and you really have a way with words...

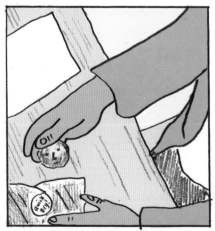

15.

An ending

A couple of days before travelling to London, I stayed at my brother's house. We'd gone out with a few of his friends.

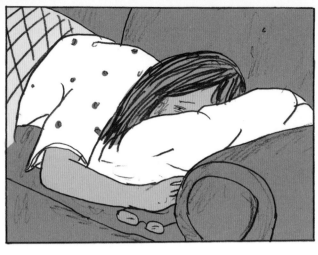

At previous film nights, Mark's housemate had chosen something indie like The Trial, La Jetée or Silent Running.

Today wasn't that kind of day...

We watched Tomb Raider.

Something dumb and distracting.

Something you didn't have to think about.

Ring! Ring!

Ring! Ring!

Hello?...
Hi dad.
Yeah. I'll
get her.

Hi dad.
20 mins?

Zoe and Julie
are home too?

Okay. See you in
a bit.

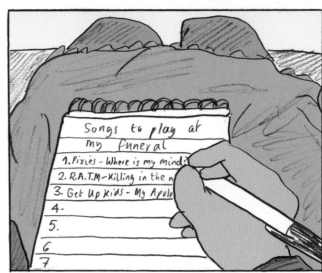

I hardly slept that night.

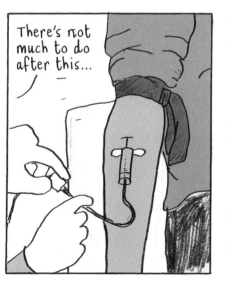

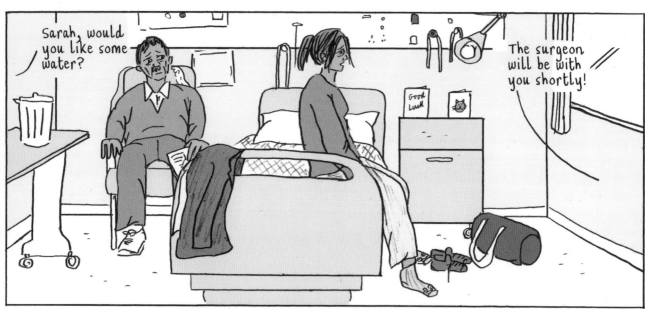

To revascularise blood flow to your brain we'll be performing cerebral bypass surgery.

What we'll be doing tomorrow is the equivalent of a coronary bypass in the heart...

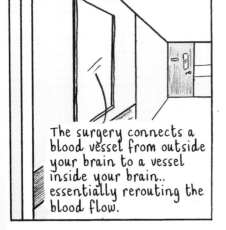

The surgery connects a blood vessel from outside your brain to a vessel inside your brain.. essentially rerouting the blood flow.

And can you remind us again about the risks involved?

Every patient is different, but many have very positive results. There are of course risks – clipping of the arteries...

..could result in a stroke during the procedure. Some patients can have a seizure during the surgery, all of which could result in some negative outcomes.

However, the chance of success is in your favour.

Now as you're 18 Sarah, you'll need to sign to give consent to the procedure and confirm you understand the risks involved.

...and that you're happy to proceed.

Okay! Well, I'll see you all bright and early in the morning!

Thank you so much.

You all get some sleep.

Thank you.

He's definitely given me more confidence, eh Ses?

Yeah... Erm. I think I'm going to read for a bit and then go to bed.

It's all going to be okay. I really believe that.

Good night, Sarah. We love you so much.

I love you, Sarah! Don't worry.

Thanks, Sam.

Sob

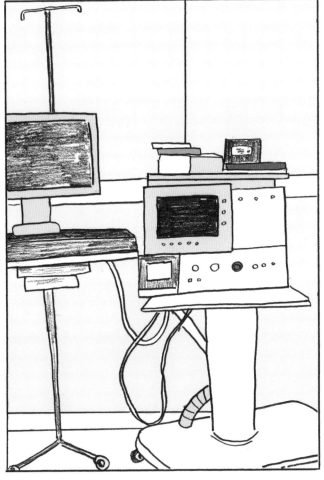

8 : 00

9 : 00

10 : 00

11 : 00

12 :00

13 : 00

14 : 00

15 : 00

16 : 00

17 : 00

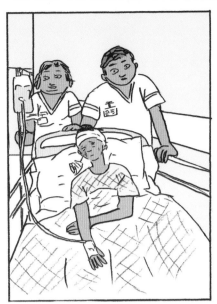
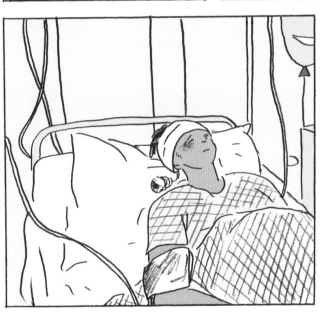

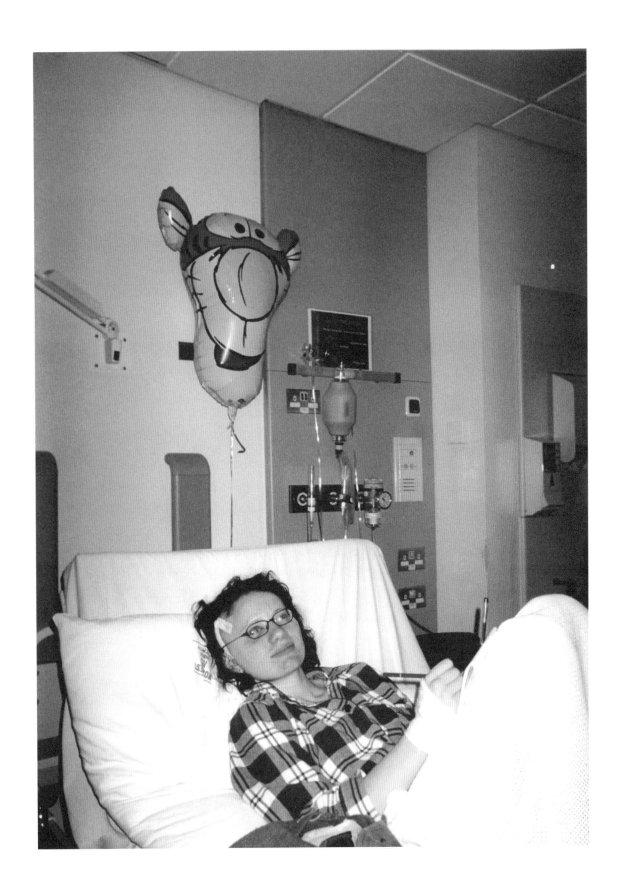

A note on Dr W:

Back in the early to late 90's there were only two consultant paediatric neurologists treating the whole of the West Midlands (total population 5.5 million). Dr W was one of those consultants.

His portrayal in my book was an honest account of mine and my parents' experiences under his care, and I am aware it is not a particularly flattering one. Whilst making my memoir I did get back in touch with Dr W, and through our correspondance I have come to terms with how complicated my condition was to diagnose, and understand the pressure Dr W was under at the time due to the staffing of the department.

Dr W knew of Moyamoya, and had treated and diagnosed Moyamoya patients prior to treating me. My condition was complex. I believe the diagnosis of Chorea and FSGS side-tracked Dr W and Dr C. And of course the Stroke revealed itself late in an MRI scan. I was not a straight forward case.

Dr W acknowledged that if he had given me an angiogram or an MRA when I was under his care, I would have been diagnosed and treated years earlier. He apologised for this. He apologised for everything. It has taken some time for me to digest and accept this information. And I have. We are only human. We all make mistakes.

A Puff of Smoke was generously supported by
an Arts Council England grant.

I'd like to express my gratitude to Medics4RareDiseases,
Dr John Connolly, Dr Sally Hulton, Dr Larissa Kerecuk,
Birmingham Children's Hospital, Great Ormond Street,
and Manchester University Medics Paediatrics Society for
helping me share my story during it's early stages.

I would like to thank the following:

Clare Bullock, Debbie Cook and Dan Franklin for your guidance
and belief in A Puff of Smoke.

My incredibly supportive, funny, kind, loving and thoughtful
family- Mum, Dad, Mark, Julie, Zoe and Sam.THANK YOU for
always being there through everything.

My best friend and husband Duncan Barrett - for helping to
get me through the making of this book, telling me to cry when I
needed to, and giving me the confidence to tell my story my way.

And lastly, but most importantly, thank you to the NHS. I don't
know what I or my family would have done without the support
of the many underpaid, overworked, kind and tireless staff within
the National Health Service who have treated and cared for me from
the age of seven.

1 3 5 7 9 10 8 6 4 2

Jonathan Cape, an imprint of Vintage,
20 Vauxhall Bridge Road,
London SW1V 2SA

Jonathan Cape is part of the Penguin Random House group of
companies whose addresses can
be found at global.penguinrandomhouse.com.

Penguin
Random House
UK

First published by Jonathan Cape in 2019.

penguin.co.uk/vintage

A CIP catalogue record for this book is
available from the British Library

ISBN 9781911214861

Printed and bound in China by C&C Offset Printing Co. Ltd

Colour reproduction by Altaimage Ltd.

Penguin Random House is committed to a sustainable future
for our business, our readers and our planet.
This book is made from Forest Stewardship Council® certified paper.

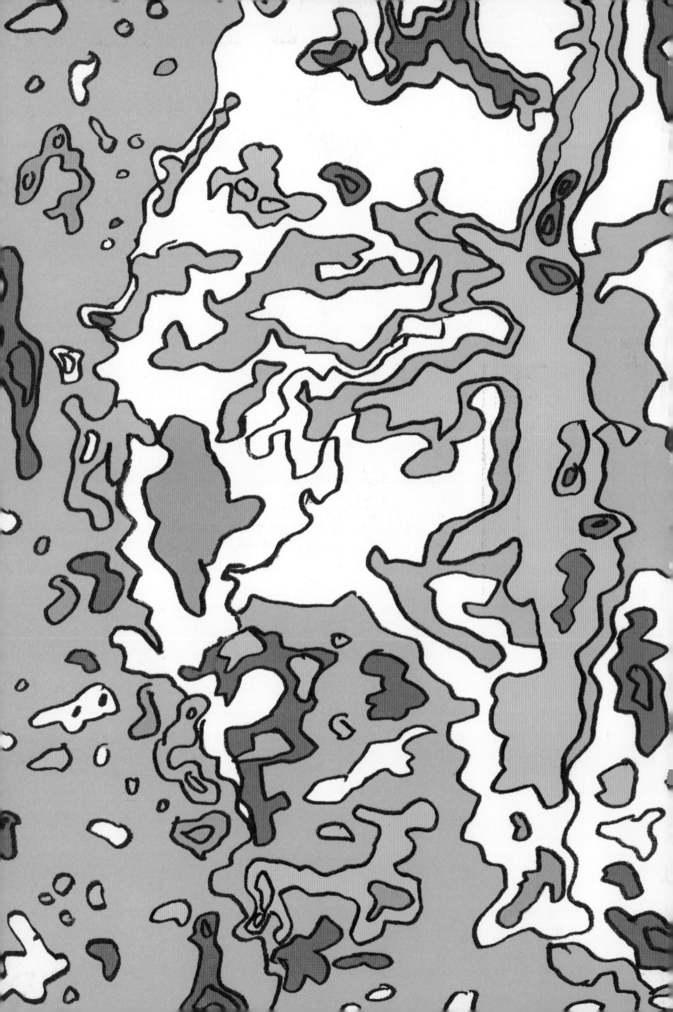